FOCUS ON CURRENT EVENTS

MINIMUM WAGE

by Eric J. Reeder

FOCUS
READERS.

VOYAGER

www.focusreaders.com

Focus Readers is distributed by North Star Editions:
sales@northstareditions.com | 888-417-0195

Produced for Focus Readers by Red Line Editorial.

Content Consultant: William Schaniel, Professor Emeritus, University of West Georgia

Photographs ©: Shutterstock Images, cover, 1, 4–5, 7, 8–9, 11, 16–17, 19, 22–23, 25, 27, 31, 34–35, 39, 40–41; Russell Lee/Library of Congress, 13; Elias Goldensky/Library of Congress, 15; Red Line Editorial, 21, 33; Lynne Sladky/AP Images, 28–29; Colin Mulvany/The Spokesman-Review/AP Images, 37; Andrew Harnik/AP Images, 43; Rich Pedroncelli/AP Images, 45

Library of Congress Cataloging-in-Publication Data
Names: Reeder, Eric J., author.
Title: Minimum wage / Eric J. Reeder.
Description: Lake Elmo, MN : Focus Readers, [2022] | Series: Focus on current events | Includes index. | Audience: Grades 4-6
Identifiers: LCCN 2021040064 (print) | LCCN 2021040065 (ebook) | ISBN 9781637390788 (hardcover) | ISBN 9781637391327 (paperback) | ISBN 9781637392331 (ebook pdf) | ISBN 9781637391860 (hosted ebook)
Subjects: LCSH: Minimum wage--Juvenile literature.
Classification: LCC HD4917 .R44 2022 (print) | LCC HD4917 (ebook) | DDC 331.2/3--dc23 eng/20211013
LC record available at https://lccn.loc.gov/2021040064
LC ebook record available at https://lccn.loc.gov/2021040065

Printed in the United States of America
Mankato, MN
012022

ABOUT THE AUTHOR
Eric J. Reeder has written several nonfiction books for students. He has also written various educational materials over the last 20 years. In his spare time, Reeder enjoys spending time with his family and friends, swimming, going to the beach, and collecting antiques.

CHAPTER 1

HARD WORK, LOW PAY

A grocery store worker has a wide variety of responsibilities. She rings up groceries for customers and bags their items. She deals with self-checkout scanners when they're having problems. She also stocks shelves and cleans up spills.

The grocery store worker has to stand during her entire shift. In many cases, she has to do the same action repeatedly and quickly. She may scan

Stocking shelves can sometimes cause injuries due to lifting, bending, and reaching.

item after item at the checkout. Or she may put can after can onto a shelf. She often stands in one small space for hours at a time. And if customers are rude to her, she must do her best to be nice.

Working at a grocery store is not easy. It does not pay much, either. In many cases, grocery store workers earn minimum wage. Minimum wage is the lowest amount that companies are allowed to pay most workers.

In 2020, approximately 247,000 workers in the United States earned minimum wage. Another 865,000 workers earned even less than the minimum wage. These low-paying jobs are not just in grocery stores. Many involve serving or preparing food. Others involve childcare, cleaning, or working at hotels.

As of August 2021, the minimum wage in the United States was $7.25 per hour. A worker who

▲ Many experts recommend that people spend no more than one-third of their income on housing.

earned that wage would make approximately $1,200 per month if she worked one full-time job. In many places, that would barely be enough to rent an apartment. So, nearly all of the worker's income would go toward housing. She would not have enough money left over to buy food. She would not have enough money to pay her electricity bills. She would not have enough money to pay her medical bills.

CHAPTER 2

EARLY ATTEMPTS AT A MINIMUM WAGE

For much of American history, there was no minimum wage. Companies could pay workers any amount, no matter how small. In the 1800s, workers began fighting for better treatment. One of their demands was higher wages. Change happened slowly. But in 1912, Massachusetts became the first state to set a minimum wage. In the following years, several other states made similar laws.

Samuel Gompers led the American Federation of Labor in the late 1800s and early 1900s. This group pushed for higher wages.

Minimum-wage laws created controversy. Opponents argued that the laws violated the Constitution. They said the laws gave too much power to the government. The US Supreme Court agreed. In 1923, the court ruled that states could not require minimum wages. As a result, all states had to end their minimum-wage laws.

In 1929, the Great Depression took hold. This crisis had a massive impact on the world's economy. In the United States, hundreds of thousands of businesses closed. Approximately 15 million workers lost their jobs. Those who were able to keep their jobs often had to accept lower wages. Many families struggled to pay for basic needs such as food and clothing. Millions of people lost their homes.

With so many people struggling, President Franklin D. Roosevelt called for bold action. In

▲ During the Great Depression, some people lived in shacks after they lost their homes.

1933, he pushed lawmakers to pass the National Industrial Recovery Act (NIRA). This law did not set a minimum wage. After all, the Supreme Court had ruled that such laws were illegal. However, the NIRA encouraged some companies to raise the amount they paid workers. As a result, some businesses began setting minimum weekly wages.

The NIRA did not last long. In 1935, the Supreme Court ruled that the law was illegal. But two years later, the Supreme Court made a different ruling about the minimum wage. This time, the court decided the state of Washington could have a minimum-wage law. This ruling reversed the court's earlier decision. It was exciting news for supporters of a minimum wage. Lawmakers began working on a **federal** law that would apply to the whole country.

In 1938, the US government set a minimum hourly wage. The law was called the Fair Labor Standards Act (FLSA). It required companies to pay certain workers at least 25 cents per hour. That wage was not enough for a person to live on.

The FLSA did not apply to many jobs that were held mostly by Black workers.

Also, the law did not apply to all workers. For many people, though, the FLSA meant they would earn more than ever before.

THE FAIR LABOR STANDARDS ACT

Originally, Roosevelt wanted the minimum wage to be 40 cents per hour. The idea of a 40-cent minimum wage was popular all around the United States. Even so, it faced opposition from several lawmakers. They argued that companies could not afford to pay workers that much. They said many companies would be forced to close.

Roosevelt could not convince enough lawmakers to support a 40-cent minimum wage. So, he agreed to a compromise of 25 cents per hour. The Fair Labor Standards Act became law on June 25, 1938. However, it affected only one-fifth of all workers. Many **retail** workers and transportation workers were not covered by the law. Farmworkers and government employees were not covered, either.

Franklin D. Roosevelt served as president from
1933 to 1945.

The FLSA did more than set a minimum wage.
It also addressed how much time people spent
working. The FLSA created an eight-hour workday.
It created a 40-hour workweek, too. If workers put
in more than 40 hours in a week, they would earn
overtime pay. For every hour of overtime, workers
would earn one and a half times their regular
wages. So, if a worker normally earned 25 cents
per hour, she would make 37.5 cents for every
hour of overtime.

CHAPTER 3

INFLATION

The price level of goods and services usually goes up a little bit every year. This increase is known as inflation. To understand how inflation works, consider its impact on a single good. A pound of sugar cost 5 cents in 1938. At that time, minimum-wage workers earned 25 cents per hour. So, in one hour, a worker earned enough money to buy five pounds of sugar. By 1942, the price of sugar had gone up to 7 cents per pound. As a

From 2020 to 2021, the price of bananas increased by 1.1 percent.

result, that same worker could not buy as much sugar. In one hour, he earned enough to buy only three and a half pounds of sugar. The worker experienced a loss in **purchasing power**.

Of course, prices increase for all goods and services, not just for sugar. That means workers have to spend more money every year to buy the same things. If workers' wages stay the same, they may not be able to afford those items anymore. For this reason, lawmakers have increased the minimum wage from time to time. In 1945, for instance, the minimum wage went up to 40 cents per hour. By 1961, it was $1.15 per hour.

Lawmakers made other updates to the FLSA in 1961. They covered more kinds of workers. The FLSA now applied to many retail workers. It also applied to many transportation workers and construction workers. Additional updates took

In 1966, the FLSA covered many jobs that were often held by Black people, including nursing home workers.

place in 1966. Even more workers were covered by the FLSA. Minimum-wage laws now applied to many government workers. The laws also applied to people who worked at hotels and on farms.

In 1968, the minimum wage went up to $1.60 per hour. This increase marked a high point for the minimum wage when adjusted for inflation. Measured in 2021 dollars, the 1968 minimum wage was worth approximately $12.38 per hour. After 1968, however, the purchasing power of the minimum wage slowly declined. Lawmakers still increased the minimum wage from time to time. But over the same period, inflation increased even faster. As a result, workers could not buy as much with the money they earned.

In 2009, the minimum wage went up to $7.25 per hour. But after that, it did not change for more than a decade. When President Joe Biden took office in 2021, it was still $7.25. This was the longest period in US history without an increase to the minimum wage. In terms of purchasing power, minimum-wage workers earned 41 percent less in 2021 than they did in 1968. As a result, many people called for an increase.

Biden supported the idea of increasing the minimum wage to $15 per hour. Many lawmakers agreed with this plan. However, other lawmakers strongly opposed it. They continued to debate the pros and cons of increasing the minimum wage.

MINIMUM WAGE TIMELINE

unadjusted wage   adjusted for inflation

CHAPTER 4

ARGUMENTS AGAINST BIG INCREASES

Today, most Americans agree that there should be a minimum wage. But many people oppose large increases to the minimum wage. These opponents point to several problems that could occur. One common argument is that large increases would lead to job losses.

Every company has expenses. For example, some money goes toward paying workers. Some goes toward buying supplies. Some goes toward

Grocery stores must pay companies to bring food to their stores.

paying rent. If the minimum wage goes up, some companies will have to pay workers more. That means companies will have less money to spend on other expenses.

However, many companies cannot cut costs on supplies or rent. For instance, a grocery store can't stop buying supplies such as food. If it did, it would have nothing to sell to customers. Similarly, a grocery store can't stop paying rent. If it did, there would be nowhere to sell the food. So, if the minimum wage goes up, the grocery store might need to find other ways to reduce costs. As a result, the store may **lay off** workers.

In 2021, the US Congress released a report. It estimated that 200,000 people would lose their jobs if the minimum wage went up to $10 per hour. The same report estimated that 1.6 million people would lose their jobs if the minimum

⬥ For many companies, workers' wages are one of the biggest expenses.

wage went up to $15 per hour. In general, small businesses would be hurt most by an increase in the minimum wage. Large businesses would not suffer as much.

Increasing the minimum wage could also lead to higher inflation, according to some **economists**. Using the previous example, suppose the grocery store does not lay off any workers. In this case, the store must find another way to pay higher wages. One way is to bring in extra money. To do so, the store may raise its prices. When companies start charging more for their products, inflation goes up.

Opponents of higher minimum wages also point out that the cost of living is different from place to place. For example, in 2021, the average

> ## THINK ABOUT IT

Find out how much a one-bedroom apartment costs in your area. If you earned the minimum wage, could you afford to pay rent? How much money would you have left over for food and other expenses?

▲ If the minimum wage goes up, some stores may replace workers with self-checkout machines.

one-bedroom apartment in New York City cost $3,800 per month. In contrast, the average one-bedroom apartment in Oklahoma City cost only $700 per month. So, what's right for one area may not be right for another. A higher minimum wage may be necessary in expensive cities. But opponents argue that it may do more harm than good in less-expensive areas.

CHAPTER 5

ARGUMENTS FOR BIG INCREASES

I n 2012, fast-food workers in New York City went on **strike**. Many of these workers were earning the minimum wage of $7.25 per hour. However, they demanded $15 per hour. In terms of purchasing power, that was even more than minimum-wage workers earned in 1968.

By 2013, similar strikes had taken place in cities across the United States. These strikes led to the Fight for $15 movement. Supporters of this

Many Black women and other women of color led the Fight for $15 movement.

movement believed the minimum wage should be a **living wage**. They argued that no one should have to work two or three jobs just to make ends meet. Instead, they believed one full-time job should be enough for a person to live on.

The Fight for $15 movement led to a major change in public opinion. By 2021, more than 60 percent of Americans believed the minimum wage should be $15 per hour. If that increase happened, at least 27 million workers would get a raise. As a result, many people would be lifted out of poverty. This change would have obvious benefits for low-income workers. But supporters of a $15 wage point out that it could also have benefits for all of society. That's because a higher minimum wage could save taxpayers money.

The US government spends billions of dollars every year on assistance programs. One program

▲ Approximately 70 percent of the people who receive government assistance with food work full-time jobs.

helps low-income families pay for food. Another program helps them pay for housing. Many economists believe these programs would become less necessary if more people earned a living wage. One study found that the government could save up to $30 billion per year if the minimum wage went up to $15 per hour.

Most studies show that increasing the minimum wage tends to cause very few job losses. In fact, some economists believe higher minimum wages can be good for companies, not just for workers. That's because higher pay often leads to higher job satisfaction. When workers are happy, they are less likely to leave their jobs. As a result, companies do not have to find and train new workers. That process is expensive.

Another argument for raising the minimum wage is that workers are likely to spend their money quickly. That's because most low-income workers cannot afford to put their money in

> **THINK ABOUT IT**

Suppose you owned a company. Would you be in favor of raising the minimum wage to $15 per hour? Why or why not?

savings. Instead, they tend to spend it on rent, food, and bills. So, the money they earn goes back into the economy right away. Supporters of higher wages argue that this extra spending improves the economy. They say a higher minimum wage helps everyone, not just low-income workers.

AMERICAN BUDGETS ◄

This chart shows how the average American spends his or her money each month.

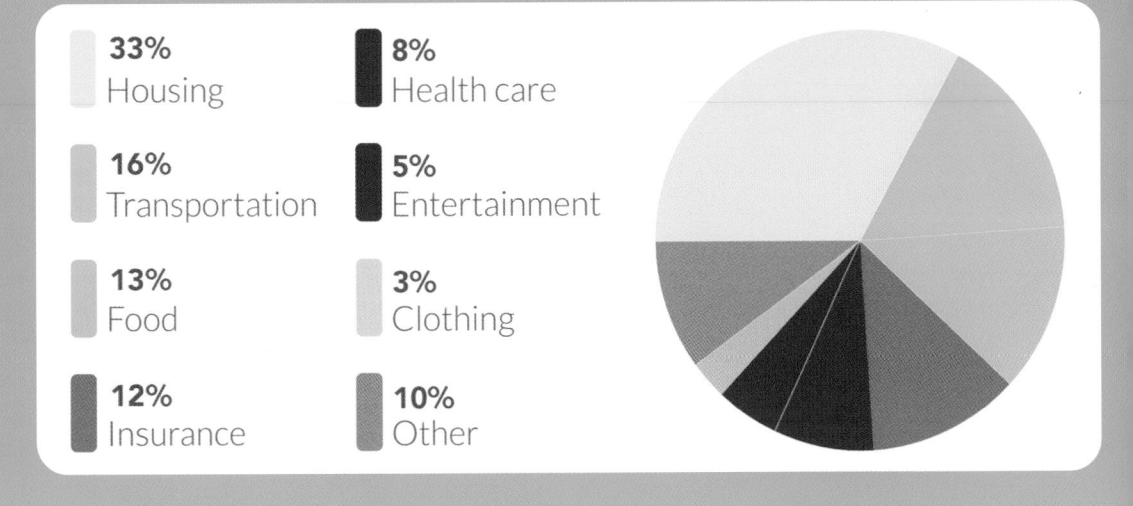

33% Housing

8% Health care

16% Transportation

5% Entertainment

13% Food

3% Clothing

12% Insurance

10% Other

CHAPTER 6

DIFFERENT RULES FOR DIFFERENT WORKERS

The federal minimum wage does not apply to all workers. In some cases, workers earn less if they have certain types of jobs. In other cases, they earn more if they live in certain places.

In 2021, the minimum wage for restaurant workers was $2.13 per hour. However, these workers receive **tips** for their service. So, their actual income ends up being higher than $2.13 per hour. Even so, restaurant workers' income can

Most restaurant workers rely on tips for the majority of their income.

be hard to predict. On busy nights, they may earn more than $20 per hour. But on slow nights, they may earn only $10 per hour. For this reason, some restaurants do not allow tipping. Instead, these restaurants pay workers living wages. The service cost for workers is included in the menu prices.

Many states, counties, and cities have their own minimum wages. These wages cannot be lower than the federal minimum wage. But they can be higher. In the state of Washington, for example, the minimum wage was $13.69 per hour as of 2021. Meanwhile, the city of Seattle had a minimum wage of $16.69 per hour. Local leaders

> ## THINK ABOUT IT

Suppose you worked in a restaurant. Would you rather earn $18 per hour and not get any tips? Or would you prefer to earn $2.13 per hour plus tips? Why?

Workers in Washington State marched in the streets in 2015 to demand higher wages.

set this level. They did so because the cost of

living is higher in Seattle than it is in other parts

of the state.

AUTOMATIC ADJUSTMENTS

Lawmakers often disagree about whether to increase the minimum wage. And if lawmakers do not make changes to the FLSA, the minimum wage stays where it is. When that happens, the minimum wage does not keep up with inflation. As a result, workers who earn the minimum wage have less purchasing power. Prices keep going up, but their wages do not.

For this reason, some economists believe the FLSA should be updated. They argue the minimum wage should automatically increase every year to match inflation. For instance, if inflation went up by 2.4 percent in a year, the minimum wage would also increase by 2.4 percent. That way, low-wage workers would

▲ In 2021, Minnesota's minimum wage automatically adjusted from $10.00 to $10.08.

maintain their purchasing power. They would still be able to buy the same number of things.

Some states already adjust wages based on the cost of living. In the early 2000s, Washington became the first. A new law required the state to look at the consumer price index (CPI) each year. The CPI tracks how much people have to pay for various goods and services. Based on this information, Washington raises its minimum wage. Over the next 20 years, several other states made similar laws. But as of 2021, the federal minimum wage did not increase automatically.

CHAPTER 7

LOOKING BEYOND MINIMUM WAGE

More than 30 million Americans live in poverty. To solve this problem, some economists argue that the government needs to do more than increase people's incomes. They say the government also needs to help control the cost of living. Rent control is one way to do that. Rent control is a set of rules meant to keep housing affordable. That way, minimum-wage

Most apartments in San Francisco, California, are rent-controlled.

workers will be able to spend more of their income on things such as food and bills.

Millions of American workers are also affected by wage theft. This happens when companies do not give full payment for the jobs workers do. For instance, a company may not pay workers for overtime. Or a company may take some of a worker's tips. Wage theft is against the law. However, few companies get caught. For this reason, many experts say the government needs to do a better job of enforcing existing laws.

Some economists argue that the idea of a minimum wage is out of date. Instead, they call for a universal basic income (UBI). In this system, the government would send monthly payments to every adult in the country. People could use the money for whatever they wanted. They would receive payments even if they did not work.

In 2020, Andrew Yang supported UBI during his unsuccessful campaign for president.

UBI would be paid for with tax increases. Compared to a minimum-wage increase, UBI would be less likely to harm companies with low-wage workers. That's because every worker and every company in the country would help pay for UBI. So, the costs would be more spread out.

Critics point out that UBI would be extremely expensive. They also argue that UBI would encourage people to stop working. However, studies show that UBI tends to have little effect on employment levels. Studies do confirm that UBI would have very high costs. But supporters argue that UBI could lead to major improvements in society. For this reason, they say, the costs are worth it.

By 2021, several cities were testing UBI. These programs did not give payments to everyone in the city. Most programs targeted low-income residents. In general, people who received UBI payments tended to become healthier. In addition, their children did better in school.

> THINK ABOUT IT

Do you think the government has a responsibility to make sure people have enough money to live on? Why or why not?

Mayor Michael Tubbs of Stockton, California, led a UBI program that resulted in higher employment.

Economists will continue to debate the pros and cons of UBI. Meanwhile, lawmakers will continue to debate the minimum wage. On the one hand, they want to make sure companies are able to stay in business. On the other hand, they want to make sure workers have a reasonable standard of living.

FOCUS ON
MINIMUM WAGE

Write your answers on a separate piece of paper.

1. Write a letter to a friend explaining the arguments for and against raising the minimum wage.

2. Do you support a minimum wage of $15 per hour? Why or why not?

3. When did the Fair Labor Standards Act become law?

    A. 1912

    B. 1938

    C. 1968

4. Why might raising the minimum wage have a greater impact on small businesses?

    A. Small businesses usually don't hire workers.

    B. Small businesses usually spend more money than large businesses.

    C. Small businesses usually have less money to spend than large businesses.

Answer key on page 48.